HAL LEONARD

CAJON METHOD

BY PAUL JENNINGS

To access video, visit:
www.halleonard.com/mylibrary

Enter Code
2905-3132-1312-0827

Cover photos by Natalie Champa Jennings

Music notation by Alex Kosak

ISBN 978-1-4950-0241-0

HAL•LEONARD®
7777 W. BLUEMOUND RD. P.O. BOX 13819 MILWAUKEE, WI 53213

In Australia Contact:
Hal Leonard Australia Pty. Ltd.
4 Lentara Court
Cheltenham, Victoria, 3192 Australia
Email: ausadmin@halleonard.com.au

Visit Hal Leonard Online at
www.halleonard.com

CONTENTS

PART 1: THE BASICS

ABOUT THE CAJON

The *cajon* is believed to have originated with the Afro-Peruvian people of coastal Peru in the early 1800s, when slave musicians, brought from West Africa, decided to use shipping crates as drums in order to continue their music and dancing traditions. The Afro-Peruvians sat on top of the crates and played with their hands to create the rhythms. Over the next 100 years, the Afro-Peruvian culture developed, and the cajon was born.

In its early years, the cajon was used to accompany the traditional Afro-Peruvian dances, such as Zamacueca, Festejo, and Lando. Other types of cajon drums also emerged in Cuba and other countries in Latin America. In the 1970s, Rubem Dantas, the percussionist for flamenco guitarist Paco De Lucia, was gifted a cajon whilst on tour in Peru. Dantas brought the cajon back to Spain and began using the instrument in flamenco music. By doing so, he began a movement that would eventually establish the cajon as a principle instrument of the flamenco tradition.

Traditional Afro-Peruvian cajons have no snare system. After the cajon reached Spain, guitar strings were fixed to the back of the playing surface (the "tapa"), resulting in a rattle on the slap tone like that of a snare drum. This became characteristic of the flamenco cajon sound. It is now common for modern cajon drums to have snare wires, or even a snare mechanism, as part of the instrument, which gives the cajon, with its powerful bass tone and snare crack, the sound like that of a drum set in a box.

You can now hear the cajon being used in a great many musical genres. Its popularity and reputation as one of the world's most versatile percussion instruments is growing faster by the day. Welcome to the wonderful world of the cajon!

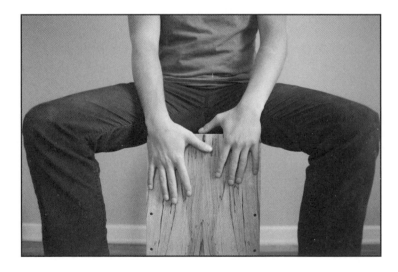

ANATOMY OF THE CAJON

The cajon is a box drum comprised of two side panels, one back panel (usually where the sound hole is located), one top panel, one bottom panel, and one front panel, which is where the cajon is played. The front panel is sometimes called the "tapa."

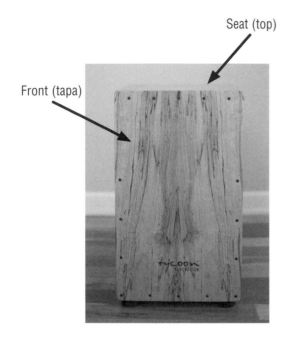

Seat (top)

Front (tapa)

Sound hole

Snare inside

Back side

PLAYING POSITION

The cajon is designed to be played on the front surface while sitting on the top. It is important to maintain a good, relaxed posture while playing. Listed below are the general guidelines for maintaining a good playing posture:

- Sit on top of the cajon, near the back, so that you have good access to the playing surface. Place your hands on the front (playing surface) of your cajon.

- Place both feet on the ground to either side of your hands.

- Try to keep your back straight but stay relaxed—don't slouch or hunch over.

- Most tones, including the bass tone, are achieved within the top eight inches of the cajon.

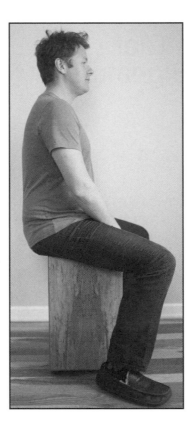
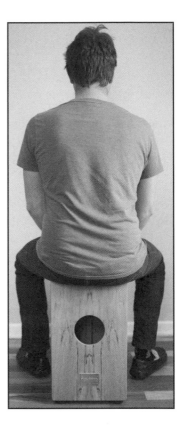

NOTATION KEY

Conventional music notation is written as notes on a staff. A staff has five lines with four spaces—one space between each line.

Five-line Staff

Barlines

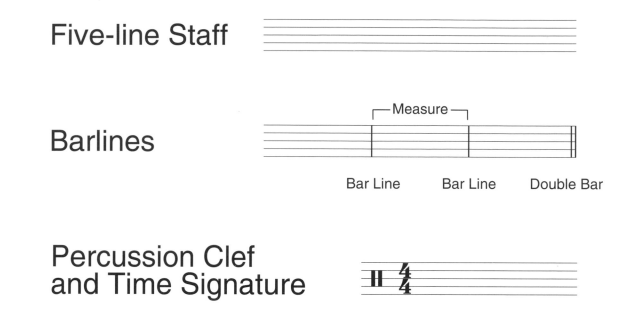

Bar Line   Bar Line   Double Bar

Percussion Clef and Time Signature

NOTATION SYMBOLS

Where a note is placed on the staff usually determines the pitch of the note. The notation used in this book for cajon is slightly different. A note's placement on the staff will determine what tone of the cajon is being used. There are also different symbols for each tone of the cajon, which will make the notation easier to follow.

Cajon Notation Legend

Bass Tone   Mid Tone   Slap Tone   High Slap Tone

Other Musical Symbols

Other musical symbols are also used in this book.

Accent: >
Accents are notes played with a greater emphasis. When you play a note with an accent symbol, you should play that note louder than the other notes.

Tie: ⌣
A *tie* is a curved symbol that ties two notes together. You play the first note and sustain it through the value of the tied note, as well.

Hands:
The letters R and L tell you which hands to use for each beat. R = right hand, L = left hand.

Important: All the lessons in this book are taught with a right-hand lead. If you are left-handed or feel more comfortable playing with a left-hand lead, feel free to reverse the hand directions.

READING NOTE VALUES

To be able to understand the lessons in this book, you will need to understand note values (how long each note lasts). Each note symbol represents a different value. A whole note lasts for one whole bar (or measure), a half note's value is half of a whole note, and a quarter note's value is a quarter of a whole note, etc. We can keep subdividing all the way down to what are called 64th notes (and more, theoretically!).

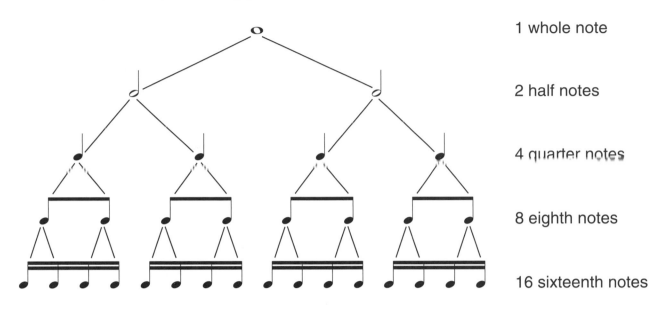

	1 whole note
	2 half notes
	4 quarter notes
	8 eighth notes
	16 sixteenth notes

The note-value tree shown above subdivides the note values down to 16th notes.

COUNTING

The majority of modern Western music is notated and counted by dividing the rhythmic pulse into groups of four, meaning four separate beats. This is counted as: "one, two, three, four." These would be quarter notes.

You can then subdivide them into eighth notes: "one – and, two – and, three – and, four – and."

And 16th notes would be counted as such: "One – e – and – a, two – e – and – a, three – e – and – a, four – e – and – a."

When playing many of the grooves in this book that are in 4/4, it's very helpful to count out all the 16th notes in your head. This will help you figure out where each hit lands.

16th Notes

In this notation, we'll use the "+" symbol in place of the word "and":

Triplets

Triplets are groups of three notes that are played in the space of two. The best way to count triplets is as follows:

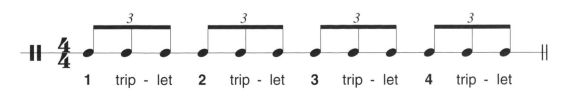

NOTE VALUE EXERCISES

These exercises will help you understand note values and get you familiar with reading the notation. The *repeat signs* (‖: :‖) tell you to play the enclosed music again before proceeding.

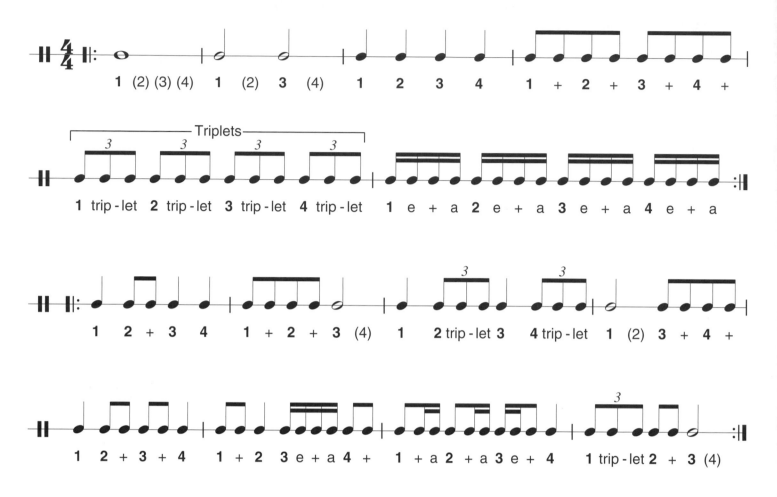

RESTS

A *rest* is a period of silence in music that is notated with a symbol that indicates the length, or note value, of the rest.

Whole Rest   Half Rest   Quarter Rest   Eighth Rest   16th Rest

Below are some rest exercises. When playing these exercises, it's helpful to count out the rhythms and say "rest" when you should rest.

Rests Exercise

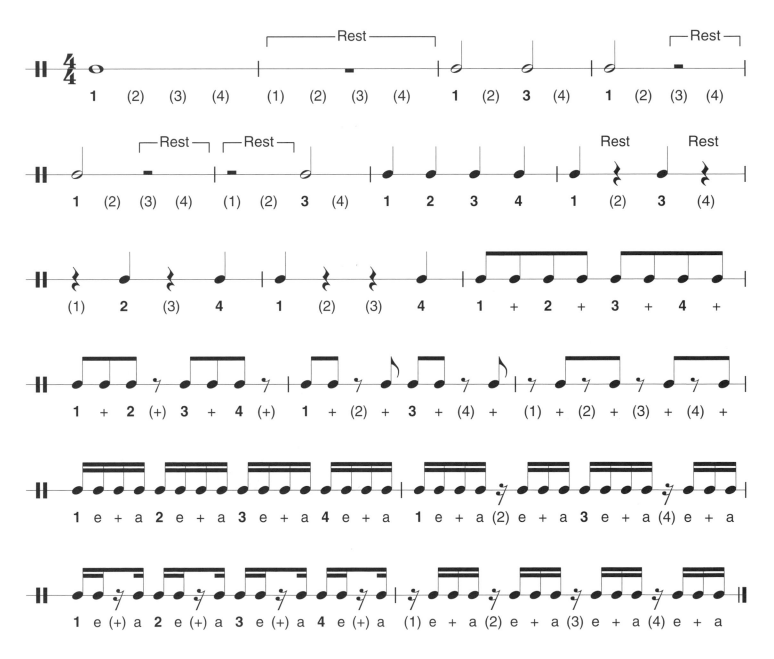

BASS, MID, AND SLAP TONES

Two of the most prominent sounds of the cajon are the bass and slap tones.

BASS TONE

 The bass tone is achieved by striking the cajon with a flat, relaxed hand within the top eight inches of the playing surface. Your fingers should face down, and the end of your wrist should be just below the top edge of the cajon. There is no need to stretch to the middle of the drum to get the bass tone. A nicer bass tone is found closer to the top.

Follow this basic exercise for the bass tone. Hit the bass tone by alternating each hand. Take it nice and slow at first.

R L R L R L R L R L R L R L R L

SLAP TONE

 The slap tone is achieved by literally slapping the top of the cajon. Your hand should strike the top edge of the cajon about halfway down your palm. Your fingers should bounce off each time, but your palm should stay on the edge.

Follow this basic exercise for the slap tone. Hit the slap tone by alternating each hand. Take it nice and slow at first.

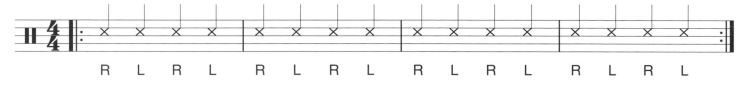

R L R L R L R L R L R L R L R L

Tips:

• Play the exercises with a metronome set to a 4/4 pattern and start slowly (50 bpm or lower).

• Gradually increase the tempo as you get more comfortable with the exercise.

HIGH SLAP TONE

 The high slap tone is achieved by striking the cajon at the top edge with the tips of your fingers. When playing slower, your fingers can stay on the cajon after you play the hit. As you play faster, you will naturally want to lift your fingers right after the hit. For right now, just try to sound a nice high slap tone that pops.

Follow this basic exercise for the high slap tone. Hit the high slap tone by alternating each hand. Take it nice and slow at first.

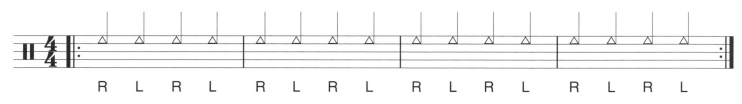

R L R L R L R L R L R L R L R L

MID TONE

The mid tone is one that you will eventually use for fills and ghost notes. It's achieved by cupping your hands and striking the cajon with the tips of your fingers five to six inches from the top of the cajon.

Follow this basic exercise for the mid tone. Hit the mid tone by alternating each hand. Remember to keep your hands cupped and take it slowly at first.

R L R L R L R L R L R L R L R L

Tip:

- It may take some time and practice to get good tones. Be patient, practice regularly, and you will have the tones down in no time.

BASS AND SLAP TONE EXERCISE

 You have now learned the four tones of the cajon and are ready to move on to some exercises and patterns. In this simple exercise, you'll practice alternating between the bass tone and the slap tone. This will help you become more comfortable playing the two tones and introduce you to playing a basic rhythm on the cajon.

Start by using only your right hand to play the bass tone and slap tone. Play one hit on each tone. Then try using only your left hand. Focus on the sound and make sure that you're getting a nice, solid bass tone and a good crack for the slap tone.

Now let's try the exercise using both hands. Play one bass tone and one slap tone using your right hand. Then play one bass tone and one slap tone using your left hand.

Repeat the pattern and try to keep it going as long as you can.

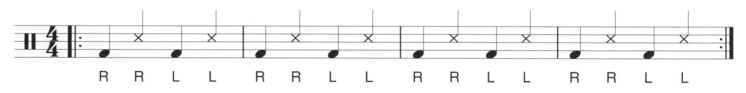

R   R   L   L   R   R   L   L   R   R   L   L   R   R   L   L

Tips:

- Use a metronome to help you keep a good tempo and build a solid sense of timing.

- Start slowly! It can take your muscle memory many repetitions to get comfortable with the pattern. Gradually increase the tempo.

- Maintain good posture.

8 TO 1 EXERCISE

The 8 to 1 exercise is great to use as both a warmup and as a way to improve your tone and technique. The exercise begins by playing eight beats with your right hand and then eight beats with your left hand. Then play seven beats with your right hand and then seven with your left hand. Keep doing this, each time taking away one beat, until you play only one beat with each hand. Then work your way back up to eight again. Keep cycling up and down from eight to one.

Use a metronome with this exercise to help keep your hits consistent and evenly spaced. This exercise is notated on the slap tone, but you can also play it on the other tones.

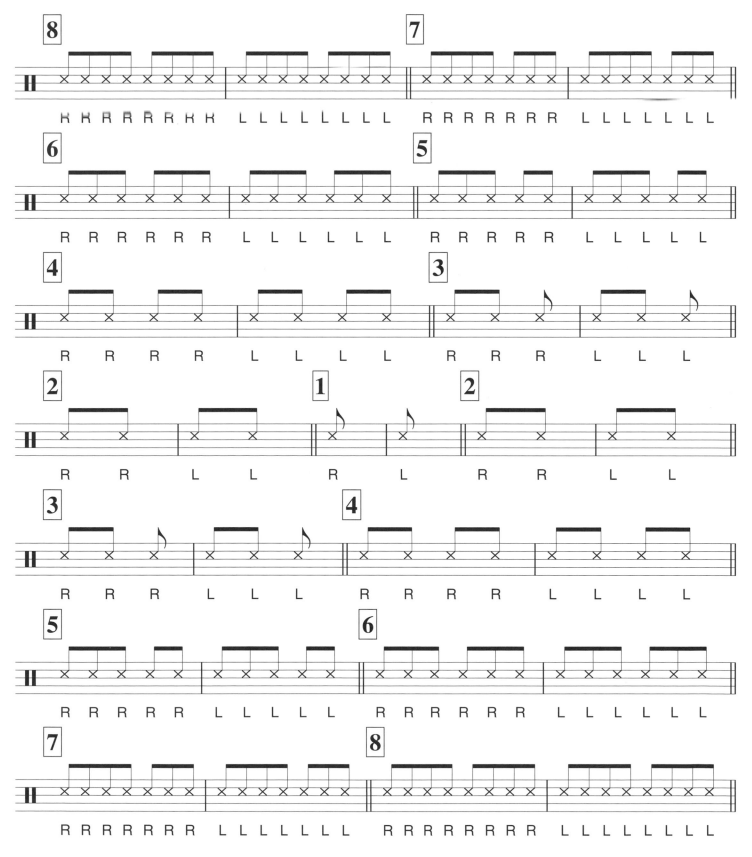

THREE-TONE EXERCISE

In this exercise, you'll introduce the high slap tone, which you learned on page 11. The exercise will give you a chance to work on three tones and also practice playing a basic pattern.

Start by using only your right hand to play the bass tone, slap tone, and high slap tone. Play one hit on each tone.

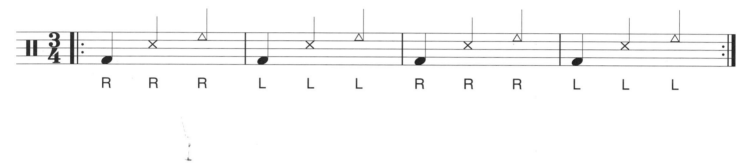

BASS/SLAP TONE DOUBLES

Now we'll try something a little more challenging. We'll begin by playing two beats with the right hand on the bass tone and then move to the left hand for two beats on the bass tone. After that, we'll move up to the slap tone, playing two beats with each hand.

Try to keep the pattern going, playing the beats evenly spaced and with the same force.

Tips:

- Always check that you are playing each tone correctly.

- If your hands are getting sore, take a break.

BASIC 4/4 GROOVE

 Now that you've learned the four basic tones of the cajon, it's time to learn your very first groove. This groove is in a 4/4 time signature, so there are four beats in each bar.

We're going to count the groove like this (read "+" as "and"): **1** + **2** + **3** + **4** +

The groove begins on beat 1 of the bar with a bass tone hit with the right hand. The next hit is on the slap tone with the left hand, which lands on the "and" just before beat 3. The next hit lands with the right hand on beat 3. Bar 2 of the groove is played the same as bar 1, with one extra hit by the left hand on beat 4.

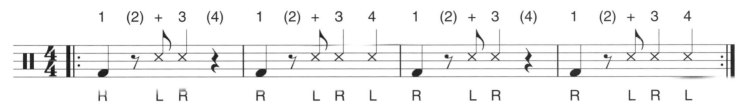

BASIC 4/4 GROOVE VARIATION

Here's a variation of the basic 4/4 groove. We're doubling up on the bass tones each measure, and we're adding another slap tone to beat 3 in measures 2 and 4.

Tips:

- Use a metronome to practice this groove. Start with a slower tempo and then increase the bpm as you feel comfortable.

- Take it slowly and don't get frustrated. With some good, solid practice, you'll have this groove down in no time.

ROCK GROOVES

 Rock is a great genre to start playing on the cajon, as many people are familiar with the sound and feel of rock music.

ROCK GROOVE 1

Count the groove like this: **1** + **2** + **3** + **4** +

This is in the 4/4 time signature and is made up of five hits before repeating the groove again. The first hit is a right-hand bass tone on beat 1 of the bar. The second hit is a left-hand slap tone on beat 2. The third and fourth hits are both right-hand bass tones, on beat 3 and the "and" of beat 3. The fifth hit is a left-hand slap tone on beat 4.

ROCK GROOVE 2

Our second rock groove uses 16th notes, so we'll count it like this: **1** e + a **2** e + a **3** e + a **4** e + a

Tips:

- Find a 4/4 rock song that you like and play along with the song by using Rock Groove 1 or Rock Groove 2.

- Check your posture.

- For a variation, try using a *high* slap tone instead of a slap tone.

USING FILLS

 Fills are what drummers and percussionists use to punctuate the end or beginning of a section, such as a verse or chorus. When used properly, fills can give a groove some nice, dynamic contrast.

Fills should be used in a way that works in the context of the music. For example, one song could call for very simple fills used sparingly, while another song could call for the use of busy fills throughout much of the song. It's hard to put down on paper exactly how one should use fills, but I would say to just use your intuition. If something sounds as though it might be too busy or unnecessary for the song, then it probably is.

ROCK FILL 1

Rock Fill 1 is in 4/4 time. We'll start by playing one bar of Rock Groove 1. In this exercise, the fill begins on beat 3 of bar 2 and is played over beats 3 and 4.

The fill is made up of four hits on the slap tone and four hits on the bass tone: RLRL – RLRL. The first hit of the fill is a right-hand slap tone on beat 3 of bar 2.

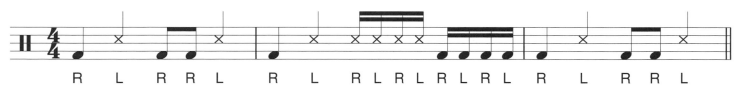

ROCK FILL 2

Rock Fill 2 is also in 4/4. We'll start by playing one bar of Rock Groove 1. The fill begins on the "a" before beat 3.

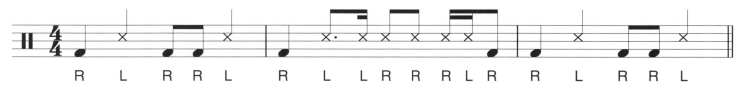

Tips:

- When you listen to a song, listen for the fills a drummer or cajon player might be using. Try to identify how and where they are using them within the song.

- Play through a rock groove and try placing the fills at different points of the bar.

GHOST NOTES

 Ghost notes are called as such because they are quiet and sometimes barely audible. We use them to give a groove some character and flavor in-between the main accented beats. Here's how they're notated:

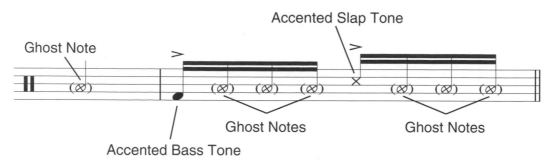

GHOST NOTE EXERCISE

In this ghost note exercise, we're going to play all the 16th notes as ghost notes on the mid tone. The bass tone and slap tone hits will be the main accented beats.

Be aware of the volume of the ghost notes compared to the main beats. There should be a clear difference in volume, with the main beats at a normal volume and the ghost notes much quieter.

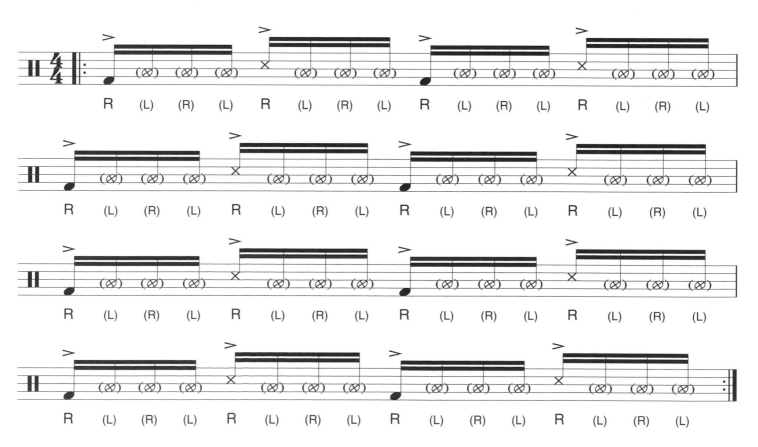

THE FLAM

The *flam* is a basic stroke that's used alongside the single stroke. Its main purpose is to create a longer-sounding note. The flam is comprised of two single hits that are played at different velocities. The loudest hit is sometimes called the *primary note*. The softer hit is called a *grace note*. The grace note should be played just before the primary note.

The grace note is not supposed to have a rhythmic value. This is because a flam can have a different feel, depending on how far apart the two strokes of the flam are spaced. It can take time to develop a good flam. You should practice playing flams with the grace note as close as possible to the primary note and also at a further distance.

Also note that the grace note and primary note are attached to each other with a slur in the notation.

FLAM EXERCISES

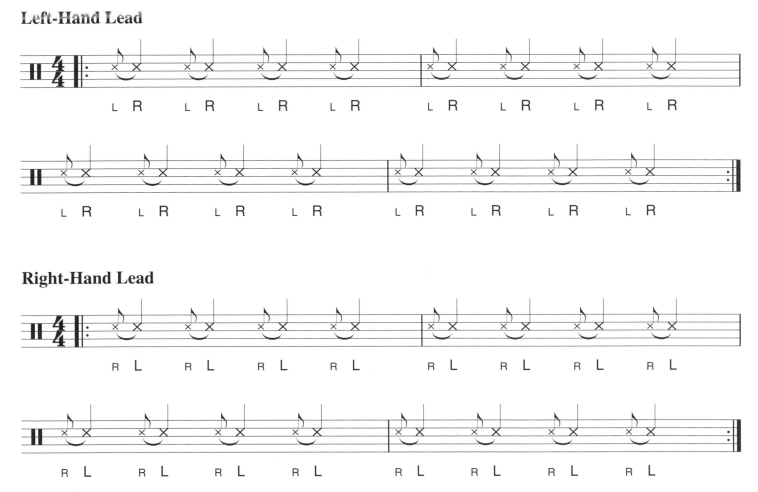

16TH-BEAT FAST ROCK

 This 16th-beat fast rock groove is called as such because it has a strong 16th-note pattern that drives it along. The 16th notes are played from right hand to left hand on the mid tone (you will play the bass and slap tone hits with the right hand only).

First try playing only the 16th-note pattern on the mid tone. When you have that down, try adding in bass and slap tones on the beats.

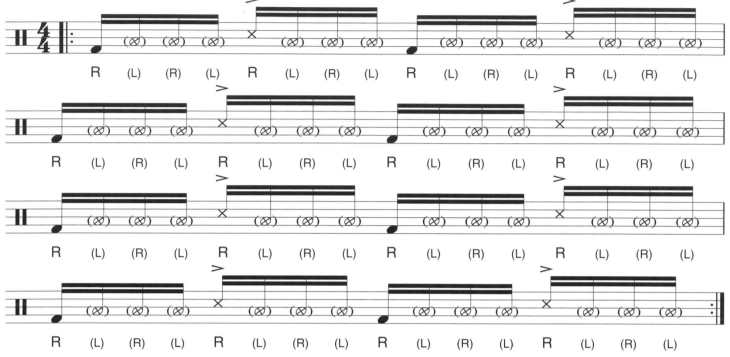

16TH-BEAT FAST ROCK VARIATION

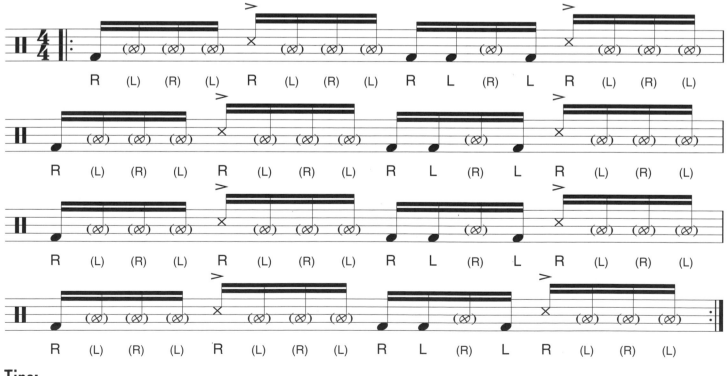

Tips:

- Even though it's called 16th-beat *fast* rock, you should try playing it slowly at first and gradually increase the tempo as you get more comfortable with the groove.

- Try finding a song for which this beat will work and play along.

PART 2: GROOVES

FUNK 1

Funk sometimes sounds a lot like rock, although the feel of the groove is different. Funk is typically focused on an on-beat/off-beat structure. Usually a greater emphasis is placed on the first beat of the bar and a solid back-beat is played on the snare (slap tone) hits.

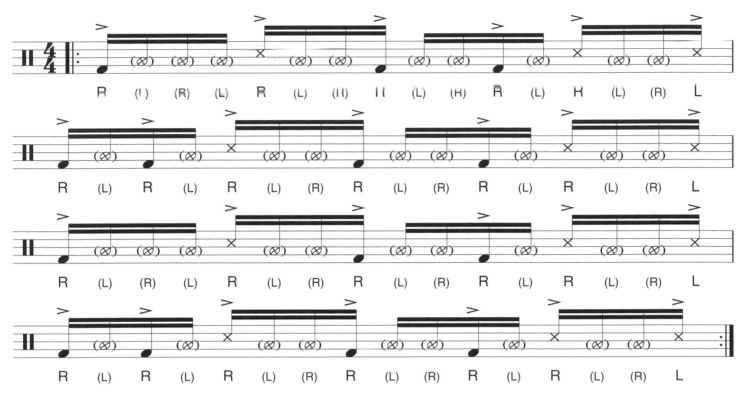

FUNK 1 VARIATION

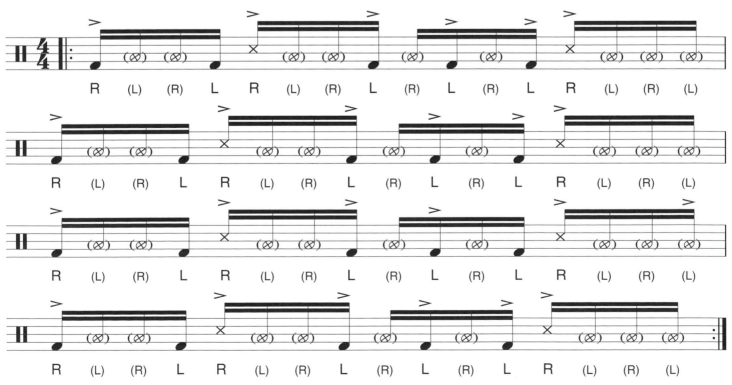

Tips:

- Listen to a funk song and try to identify the unique characteristics of the groove. Pay close attention to how it differs from rock music.

- Try blending Funk 1 and its variation together by switching between the grooves.

AFRO-PERUVIAN GROOVES

Peru, particularly the Afro-Peruvian tradition, is said to be where the cajon has its origins. This is why it's nice to have at least a basic understanding of some Afro-Peruvian rhythms.

FESTEJO

This festejo groove is one of the most popular Afro-Peruvian grooves and is counted in 12/8. This means that there are 12 beats in the bar, counted as eighth notes.

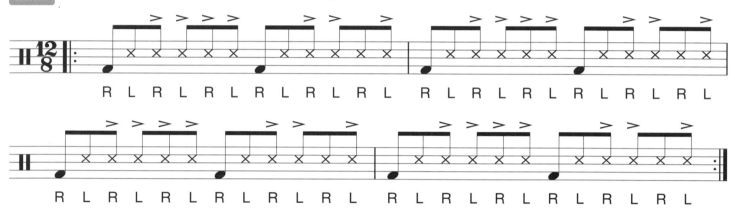

LANDO

The lando is another popular Afro-Peruvian groove. This one is counted in 6/4.

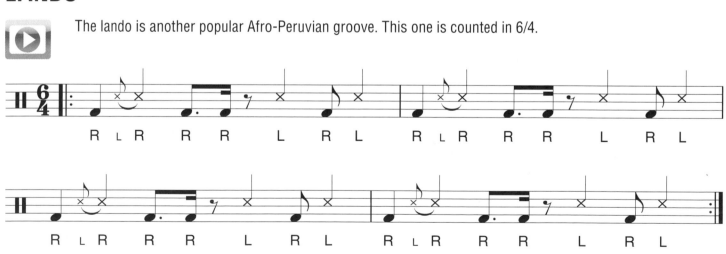

Tip:

- With Afro-Peruvian grooves, it is important to know the correct feel of the music. Try to find some Afro-Peruvian music and listen to how the instruments work within the rhythm.

LATIN AMERICAN GROOVES

SAMBA

Samba is a type of music from Brazil. It has its roots in Africa and is recognized worldwide as a symbol of Brazilian culture.

CUT TIME

Samba is traditionally notated in what is called *cut time*. This basically means that the bar is cut in two, so a bar of 4/4 would become a bar of 2/2. Samba is usually played at a fast tempo, so cut time is used to make the notation easier to read at a faster tempo.

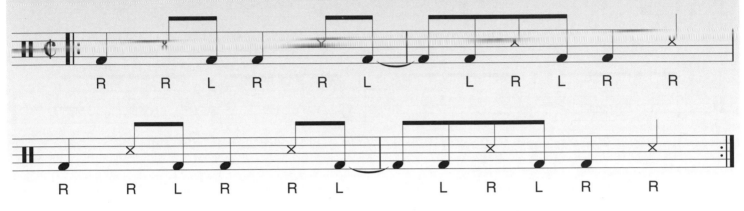

MOZAMBIQUE

Mozambique is a type of music from Cuba, particularly the Afro-Cuban tradition. Pay particular attention to the ride cymbal pattern, which we play on the high slap tone of the cajon.

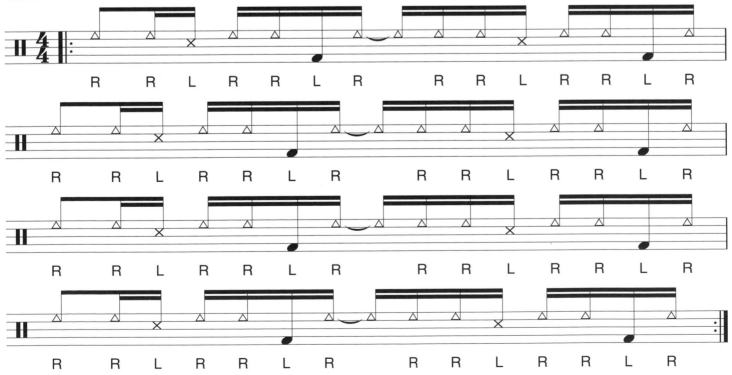

23

FLAMENCO RUMBA

Flamenco is a style of music and dance that originated in Spain. The cajon is a central part of most of today's flamenco ensembles and provides the rhythmic foundation for many of the songs and dances.

FLAMENCO RUMBA 1

Here we'll learn a flamenco-style rumba groove. There are many other types of rumba, including Cuban rumba, African rumba, and rumba dance.

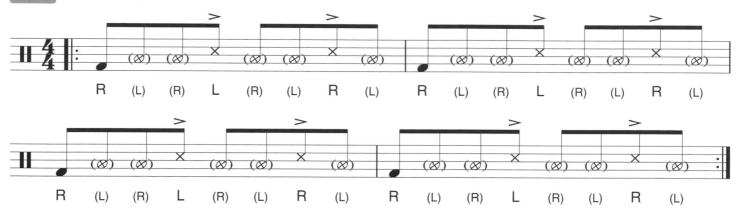

FLAMENCO RUMBA 2

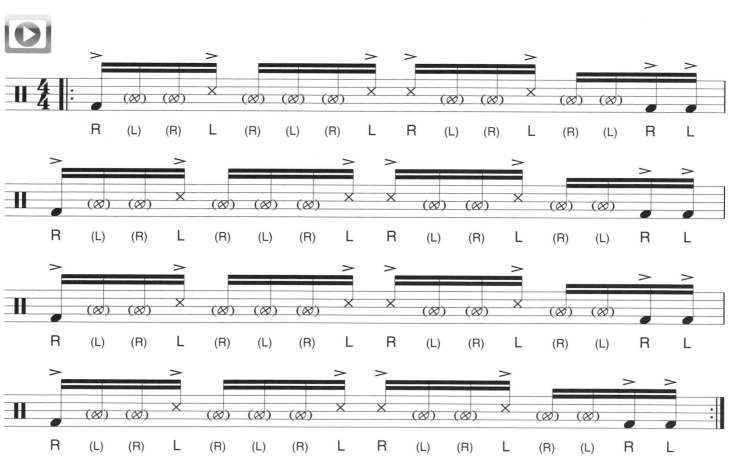

Tip:

• When you feel comfortable, try combining the rumba patterns by playing a few bars of one and then switching to the other and back again.

FUNK 2

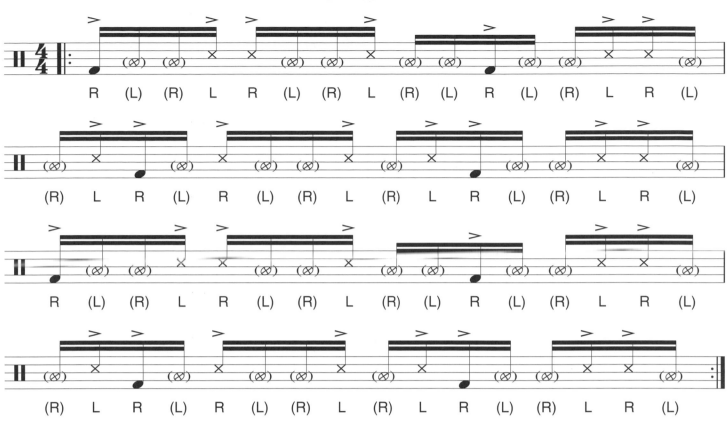

SWING

With this basic swing rhythm, we are only scratching the surface. Swing grooves have a consistent ride cymbal part, which is the groove's foundation. We'll play the ride pattern on the high slap tone.

When you feel comfortable with this groove, feel free to play around with the bass and slap tone hits while keeping the ride (high slap tone) part consistent.

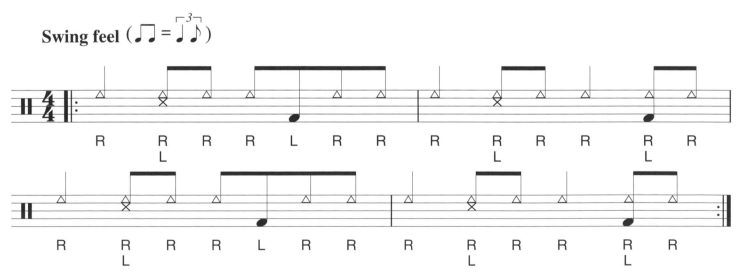

TRAIN BEAT

 The train beat is widely used across many genres of music—from country and bluegrass to Scottish and Cajun. It's called a "train beat" because it's thought to sound like a train coming down the tracks.

The rhythm consists of the hands playing constant 16th-note ghost notes. It should be counted as: **1** e + a **2** e + a **3** e + a **4** e + a.

The main accented bass tone hits land on beats 1, 2, 3, and 4. The main accented slap tone hits land on the "+" ("and") of each beat and the "e" of beat 4. The other hits are played at a softer volume, with the left hand landing on the "e" and "a" of the beat.

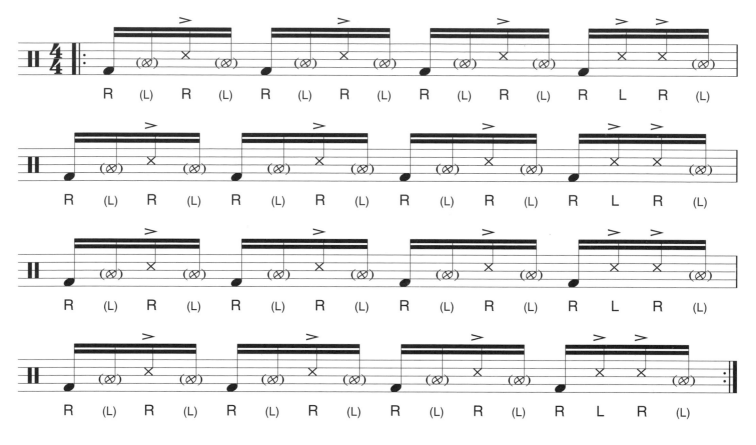

Tips:

- The train beat is quite simple in form but can sometimes take some practice to get the correct feel.

- The main bass and slap tone hits land on the down- and upbeats of each bar, respectively.

- Make sure to accent the bass and slap tones when you see the accent symbol.

BLUES SHUFFLE

The blues is a genre of music that most of us will be familiar with. Blues music usually follows a simple chord and rhythmic pattern. Blues can have a *straight feel* or a *shuffle feel*. Here, we are going to learn some blues shuffle grooves.

BLUES SHUFFLE 1

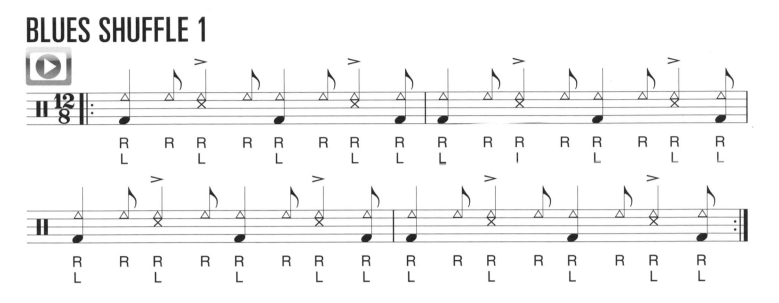

BLUES SHUFFLE 2

Shuffle feel

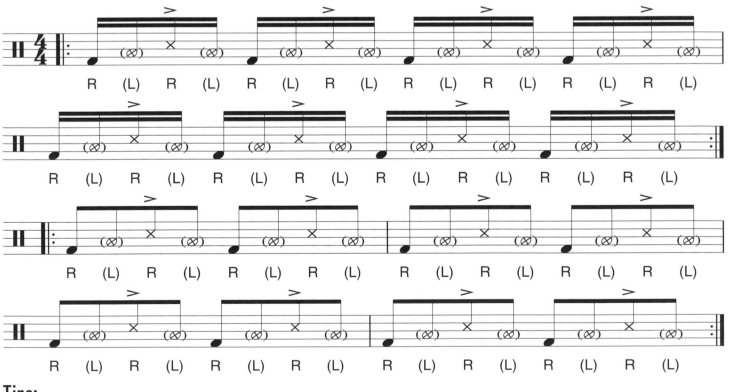

Tips:

- Remember to maintain the shuffle feel. Know the difference between playing straight versus playing a shuffle groove.

- Find a blues song with the same type of groove and try playing along.

REGGAE

 The rhythmic feel of reggae music is very distinctive. Unlike conventional rock music, there is usually no bass tone hit on beat 1 of the bar. The main bass tone hit of a reggae groove usually lands on beat 2 of the bar. There is also usually a strong hi-hat pattern, which, on the cajon, we'll play on the high slap tone.

Note that the 16th notes here are shuffled, or swung.

REGGAE 1

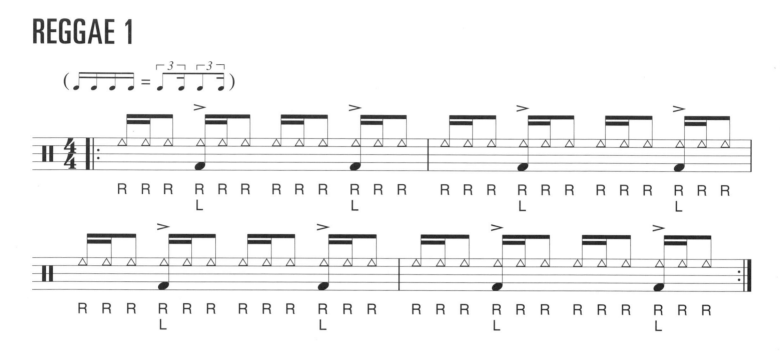

REGGAE 2

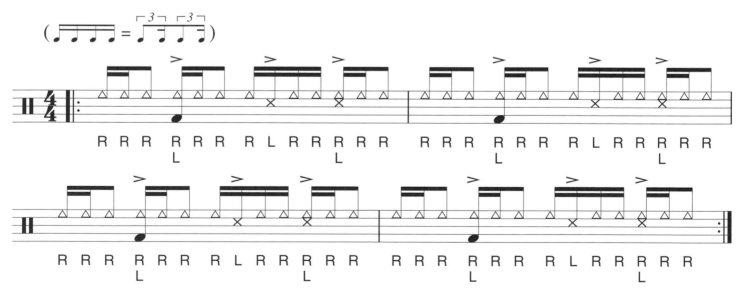

WALTZ AND 3/4 GROOVE

The 3/4 time signature is most commonly associated with the waltz but is now widely used in popular music, as well. In 3/4 time, there are three beats in the bar. This is indicated by the top number in the time signature (3). The "4" on the bottom indicates that you are counting in quarter notes.

WALTZ

This is a traditional waltz groove. It's a good introduction to playing in 3/4 time.

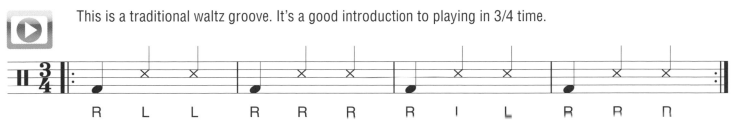

3/4 ROCK GROOVE

Now we'll take things a step further and learn a rock groove in 3/4.

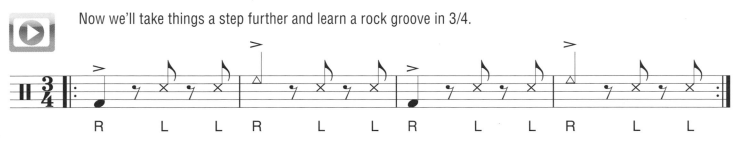

Tips:

- Set your metronome to 3/4 time and take it slow until you become familiar with the 3/4 time signature.

- Try to find a song in 3/4 and play along. Playing along to real music is invaluable and will make you a better musician all around.

MIDDLE EASTERN

This is a groove that you will hear many variations of in Middle Eastern and North African cultures. All of the high notes are played with the high slap tone.

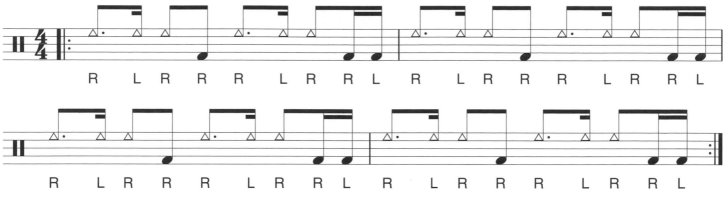

TANGO

The tango is thought to have originated in Argentina but is now widely played in many Latin cultures, including flamenco. This tango groove has a distinctive feel because there is no bass tone hit on beat 1. It's good to still count beat 1 in your head, however.

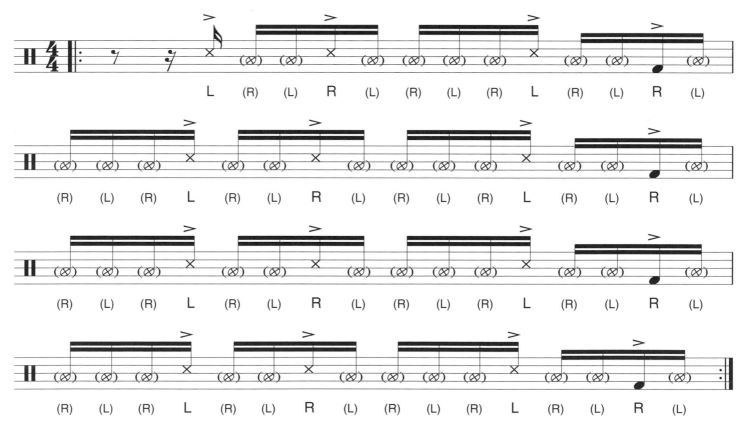

SLOW ROCK

 Here we'll look at some slow rock grooves. These feature a 16th-note hi-hat pattern, which we'll play on the high slap tone.

It's helpful to count the pattern as: **1** e + a **2** e + a **3** e + a **4** e + a. The 16th-note hi-hat pattern will be played on all of those hits.

SLOW ROCK 1

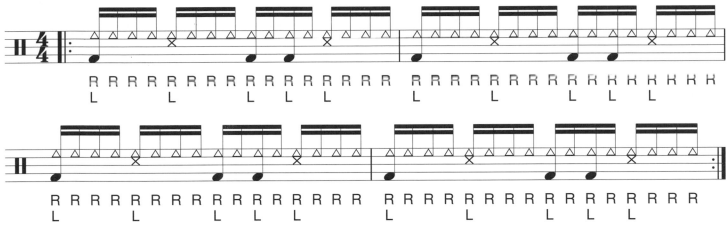

SLOW ROCK 2

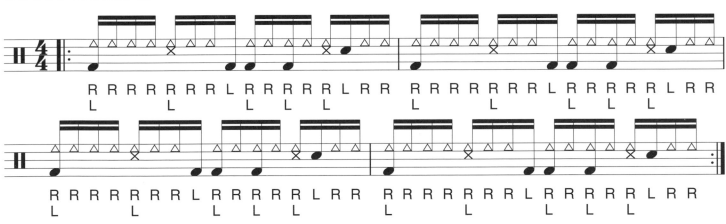

Tips:

- Remember to count the grooves as: **1** e + a **2** e + a, etc.

- These grooves are good for helping you to achieve a greater independence of your limbs.

FLAMENCO BULERIAS

 Bulerias is a popular type of flamenco music. It's unique from Western music because it's in a 12/8 time signature. This means that we have 12 beats in each bar, which are counted as eighth notes.

The other unique part of this style is that we begin the groove on beat 12 of the bar. The main accented hits fall on beats 3, 6, 8, 10, and 12. Before learning the groove, try counting it out loud and clapping your hands on the accented beats:

12 – 1 – 2 – **3** – 4 – 5 – **6** – 7 – **8** – 9 – **10** – 11 (Repeat)

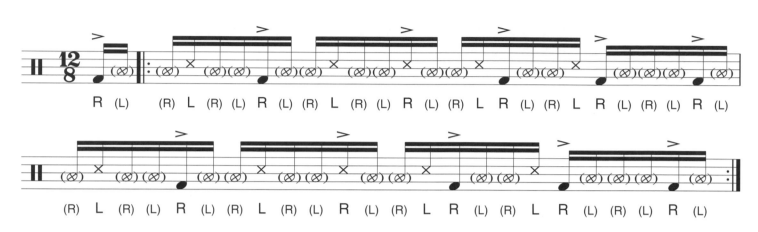

Tips:

- Try clapping out the accents of this groove before playing it.

- Find some Bulerias music and try to identify the accents.

- Don't get frustrated! This style of flamenco has a non-conventional feel, so it may take some time before you get it down.

PART 3: ADVANCED TECHNIQUES

CHANGING THE PITCH OF YOUR CAJON

At the beginning of this book, we learned the main four tones of the cajon. Those tones are used most of the time when playing grooves. It is possible, however, to play additional tones on the cajon with the use of a common technique called the *foot slide*.

Many cajon players use the foot slide to embellish grooves and/or when playing fills and solos. It's a great way to get more out of your cajon and really impress your audience.

FOOT SLIDE

Begin with your foot at the bottom of the cajon, with your heel touching the face. Now, slide your heel up the front surface of the cajon while playing the mid tone—then back down again. Listen for how the pitch of the cajon changes.

It doesn't matter which foot you use; use what feels most comfortable. You'll get the best results from playing the mid tone when using the foot slide, but you can also try using other tones, as well.

To indicate when to use the foot slide, you'll see an arrow below the notation. When the arrow points up, your foot should slide up the cajon; when it points down, your foot should slide down the cajon.

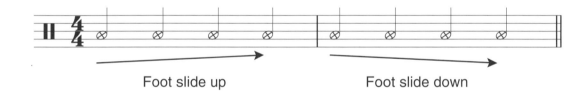

Foot slide up   Foot slide down

Now experiment with sliding your foot up and down the cajon while playing. Try different tones just to see how it sounds on your cajon. Different cajon models will react differently to the foot slide.

FOOT SLIDE EXERCISES

 Here we'll work on our foot slide technique. Make these exercises part of your practice routine to ensure that your foot slide is strong.

EXERCISE 1

In this exercise, you'll play four quarter-note beats with the right hand while sliding your foot up the cajon. Then, you'll play four quarter-note beats while sliding your foot back down. Repeat this with your left hand.

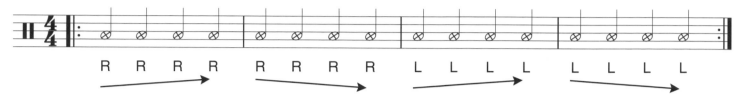

EXERCISE 2

In this foot slide exercise, we'll alternate hands from right to left, playing eight beats with the foot going up and eight beats with the foot going down.

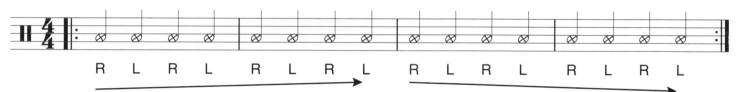

EXERCISE 3

In the final foot slide exercise, we'll play doubles: two beats with each hand with the foot at the bottom of the cajon and two beats with each hand with the foot at the top of the cajon.

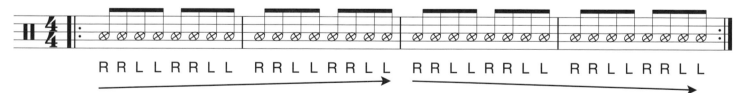

Tips:

- If your leg starts to get tired, take a break. You don't want to strain a muscle.

- Try combining the exercises.

GROOVES WITH PITCH CHANGE

We're now going to learn some grooves that incorporate the foot slide. If it helps, first learn the groove, without using the foot slide, and then add it in when you feel comfortable.

ROCK WITH PITCH CHANGE

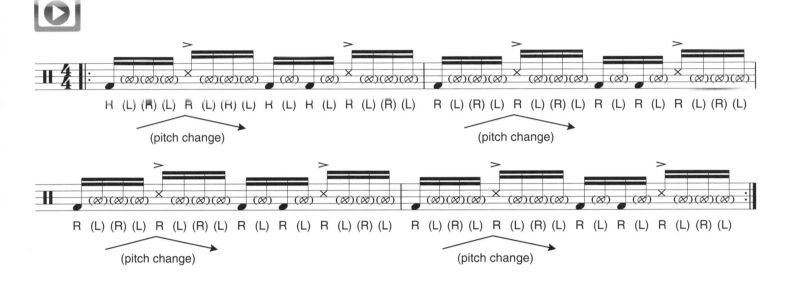

FUNK WITH PITCH CHANGE

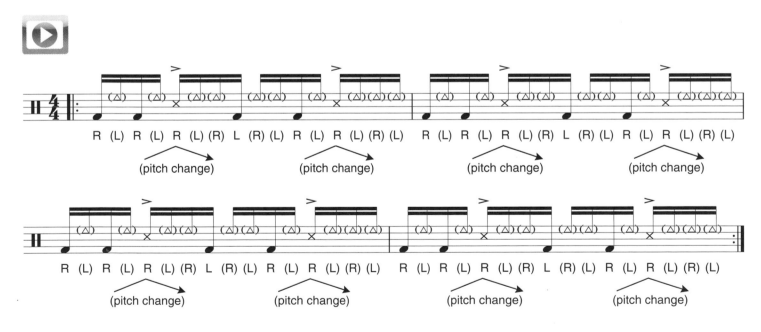

FINGER DOUBLES

 It's very common for cajon players and percussionists to use their fingers for certain techniques. Now we're going to learn how to play a common rudiment with the thumb and fingers that can be applied to many grooves and fills.

The finger doubles technique simply involves playing two hits on each hand by using a rolling technique with the thumb and fingers. The first hit is with the thumb on the right hand. Next, flick your wrist to strike the cajon with the tips of the middle and ring finger on the same hand. The two hits are repeated on the left hand, in *reverse order* (fingers first and then thumb), and we continue the cycle.

First, experiment with each hand to get the correct technique. Then, begin alternating between hands. Take it as slowly as you need to. With this type of technique, practice and repetition will make you better and faster.

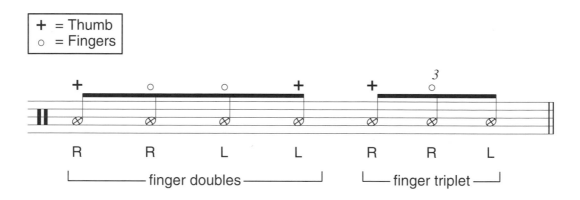

FINGER DOUBLES EXERCISE

Play this exercise slowly with a metronome and gradually increase the speed as you get more comfortable with the technique.

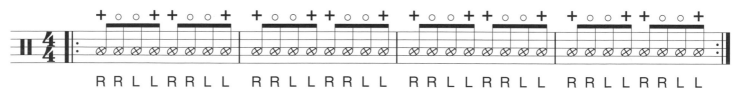

Tips:

- Some players also incorporate the pinky finger for the second hit.

- This type of technique will only get better with practice and repetition.

GROOVES WITH FINGER DOUBLES

Now let's learn some grooves that incorporate the finger doubles technique. In these grooves, we'll be introducing 32nd notes, which are simply twice as fast as 16th notes. All of the finger doubles hits will be played with 32nd notes.

ROCK WITH FINGER DOUBLES

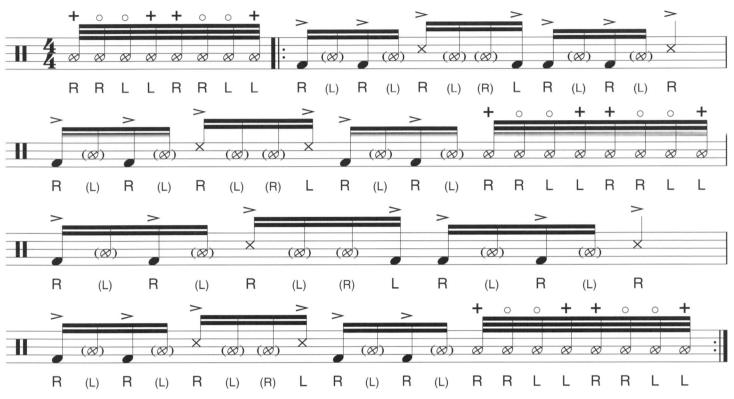

RUMBA WITH FINGER DOUBLES

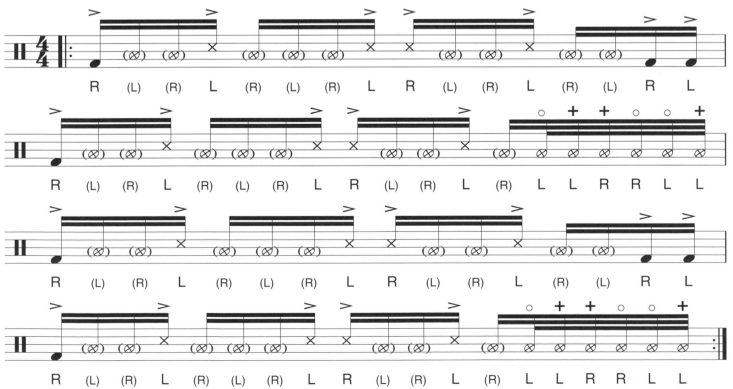

FINGER TRIPLET

 Like finger doubles, the finger triplet is a technique that can be used in many grooves and fills. The first two notes of the triplet are played with the thumb and middle/ring fingers of the right hand respectively. The third note of the triplet is usually played with either a bass tone or a slap tone.

The triplet begins on the thumb of the right hand. Then the wrist rolls to the next hit, which uses the middle finger and ring finger (and pinky finger, if you choose) at the same time. All of the power for the first two hits should come from the wrist's turning motion.

The left hand will play the third hit to finish the triplet.

FINGER TRIPLET EXERCISE

Play this exercise slowly with a metronome and gradually increase the speed as you get more comfortable with the technique. As you build speed, you'll begin to feel your right hand falling into a natural rolling motion.

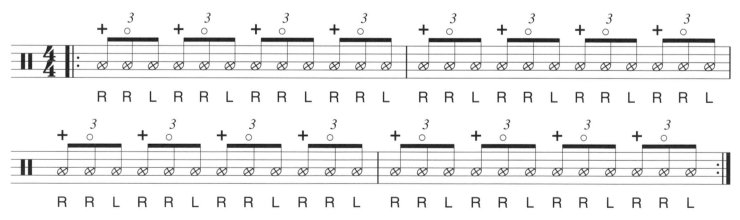

REVERSE FINGER TRIPLET

The reverse finger triplet technique can be very effective for embellishing grooves and making them sound impressive. This time, the triplet begins with the right hand playing a single mid tone. The next note is played with both the middle finger and ring finger of the left hand. Your left wrist should then twist up to play the final hit with the thumb.

REVERSE FINGER TRIPLET EXERCISE

In this exercise, we'll play a single hit on the bass tone and then a slap tone.

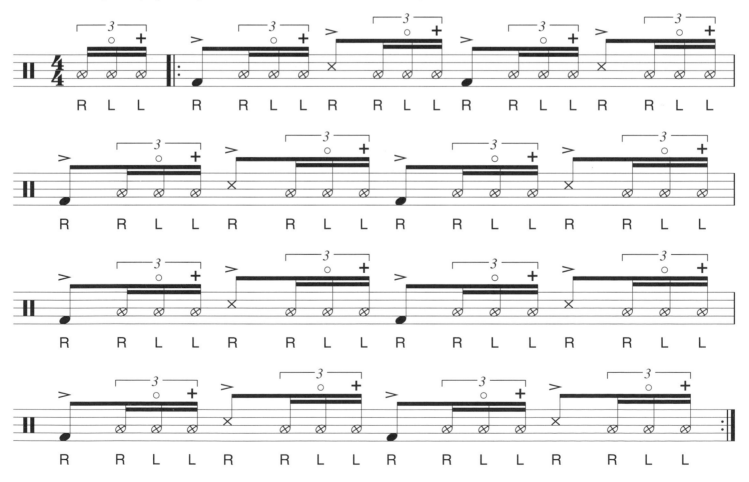

PLAYING CLAVE

Clave is a rhythmic pattern that is used as a tool to keep a band or group of drummers playing in time with the organized rhythms. In an ensemble playing Latin or Cuban music, there will almost always be a musician playing the clave on two sticks, which are simply called "claves." The ensemble must listen to and play against the clave throughout a piece of music.

Clave is used in musical traditions from Afro-Cuban to Afro-Brazilian. There are two main types of clave: *son* and *rumba*. They both follow a five-note pattern but each give a different feel, depending on where the notes and rests fall in the bar.

SON CLAVE

The most common clave used in popular Cuban music is the son clave, which was named after the son genre of music. The son clave has two forms: 3-2 and 2-3.

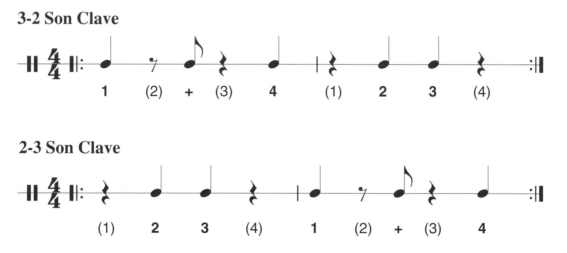

RUMBA CLAVE

The rumba clave is the other main type of clave and is used primarily in Cuban rumba music. It also has two forms: 3-2 and 2-3. Note that the rumba clave is the same as the son clave, apart from one note, which gives it a totally different feel.

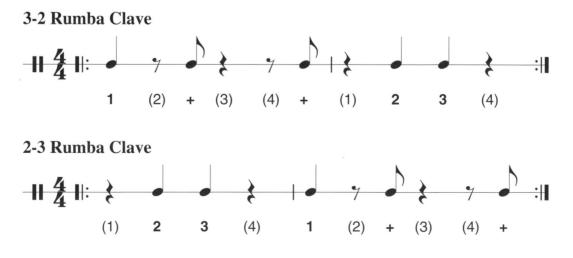

Tips:

- Clap out both the son clave and the rumba clave and become familiar with the feels and differences.

- Play along to a recording of a clave.

PARADIDDLE

 The paradiddle is one of the most common drumming rudiments and is very effective when used on the cajon. The pattern goes: RLRRLRLL. It repeats over and over.

BASS TONE PARADIDDLE

R L R R L R L L   R L R R L R L L

BASS AND SLAP TONE PARADIDDLE

R L R R L R L L   R L R R L R L L

HAND-SWITCH PARADIDDLE

R L R R L R L L   R L R R L R L L

Tips:

- Practice these exercises with a metronome, starting at a slow tempo. Gradually increase the tempo as you feel comfortable.

- When playing paradiddles, try placing accents in different places.

USING A CYMBAL WITH YOUR CAJON

Nowadays, it's common for players to add other percussion to their cajon setup. One of the most common additions to a cajon setup is a cymbal.

There are two main ways that you can use a cymbal with your cajon. The first is to hit the cymbal to punctuate points in the music, such as the beginning or end of a measure. We'll call this a cymbal "crash." The second is to use the cymbal as a "ride." When we do this, we'll play rhythmic patterns that belong to a particular groove.

If you're using the cymbal as a crash, I would recommend using a thinner weighted cymbal, such as a thin crash or a splash cymbal. This is because you'll be using your hand to hit the cymbal.

If you're using the cymbal as a ride, I would recommend using a slightly heavier cymbal, such as a crash/ride cymbal or a heavier crash. That way, you can play ride patterns on the cymbal, as well as using it as a crash.

If you're using your cymbal to play ride patterns, you'll need a brush or a stick. I would recommend a brush because it will be generally more appropriate for the volume of the cajon and you can also use a brush on your cajon.

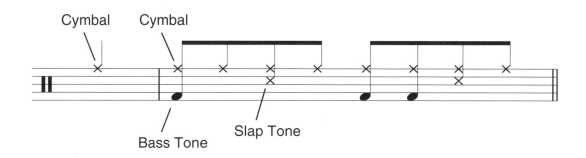

GROOVES WITH A CYMBAL

Now let's try incorporating the cymbal into some grooves.

ROCK WITH A CYMBAL

First, here's a rock groove. It's commonly played on a drum set.

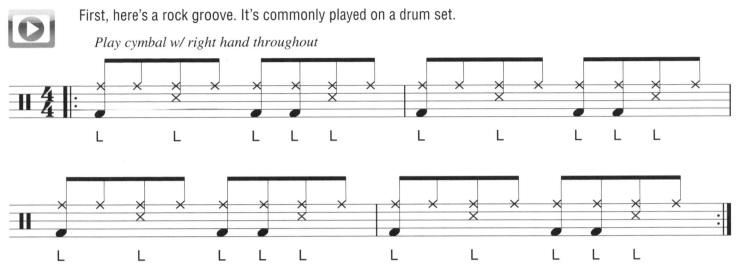

SWING WITH A CYMBAL

Now try this swing groove with a cymbal. Remember to shuffle the eighth notes.

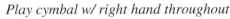

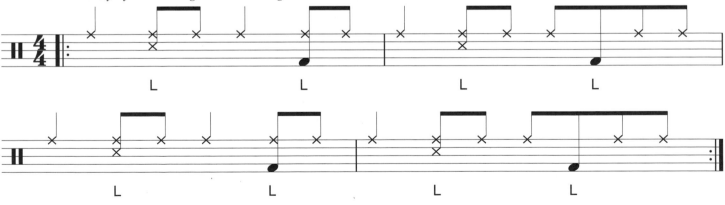

PLAYING WITH BRUSHES

 Using brushes on the cajon is becoming more and more commonplace. This is because brushes sound great on the cajon and will add a whole new dimension to your playing. Many drummers use brushes on their drum set, but the technique for holding brushes for the cajon is slightly different.

In the resting position, both brushes should be pointing down towards the floor. The brush handle should be placed in-between the middle finger and the ring finger. The index finger should lightly curl around the middle part of the handle, and the thumb should be lightly pressed against the upper part of the handle to keep the brush steady.

HOW TO USE THE BRUSHES

When playing with brushes, almost all of your power should come from your wrists and your middle finger. It's kind of a joint effort between the two, and how much wrist you use versus the middle finger largely depends on how hard you are playing. The arm can also come into play when playing a very powerful hit.

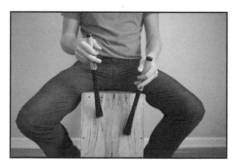

BRUSH EXERCISE AND GROOVES

This simple brush exercise will help you get comfortable with playing your cajon with brushes.

(w/ cajon brushes)

R L R L R L R L R L R L R L R L

ROCK GROOVE WITH BRUSHES

Now let's try a simple rock groove with brushes.

(w/ cajon brushes)

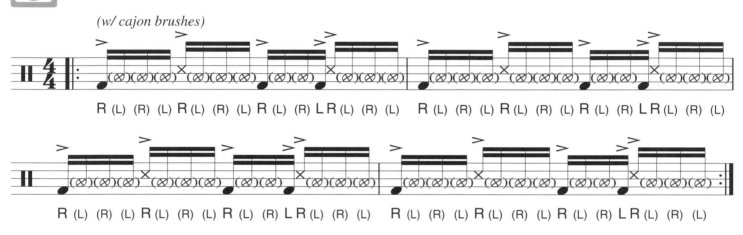

R (L) (R) (L) R (L) (R) (L) R (L) (R) L R (L) (R) (L)   R (L) (R) (L) R (L) (R) (L) R (L) (R) L R (L) (R) (L)

R (L) (R) (L) R (L) (R) (L) R (L) (R) L R (L) (R) (L)   R (L) (R) (L) R (L) (R) (L) R (L) (R) L R (L) (R) (L)

TRAIN BEAT WITH BRUSHES

The train beat is frequently played with brushes. Try this one with both your hands and with brushes to hear the difference.

(w/ cajon brushes)

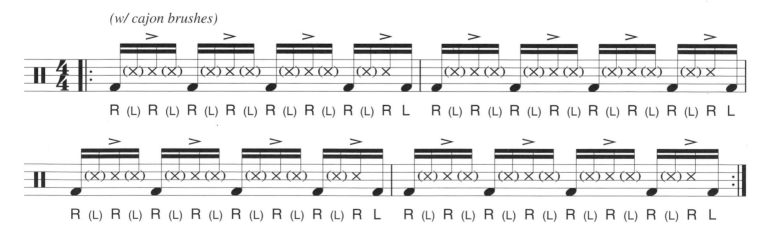

R (L) R (L) R (L) R (L) R (L) R (L) R (L) R L   R (L) R (L) R (L) R (L) R (L) R (L) R (L) R L

R (L) R (L) R (L) R (L) R (L) R (L) R (L) R L   R (L) R (L) R (L) R (L) R (L) R (L) R (L) R L

CAJON FINALE

(BY PAUL JENNINGS AND ALEX KOSAK)

Now we'll put together just about everything that we've learned into one big finale.

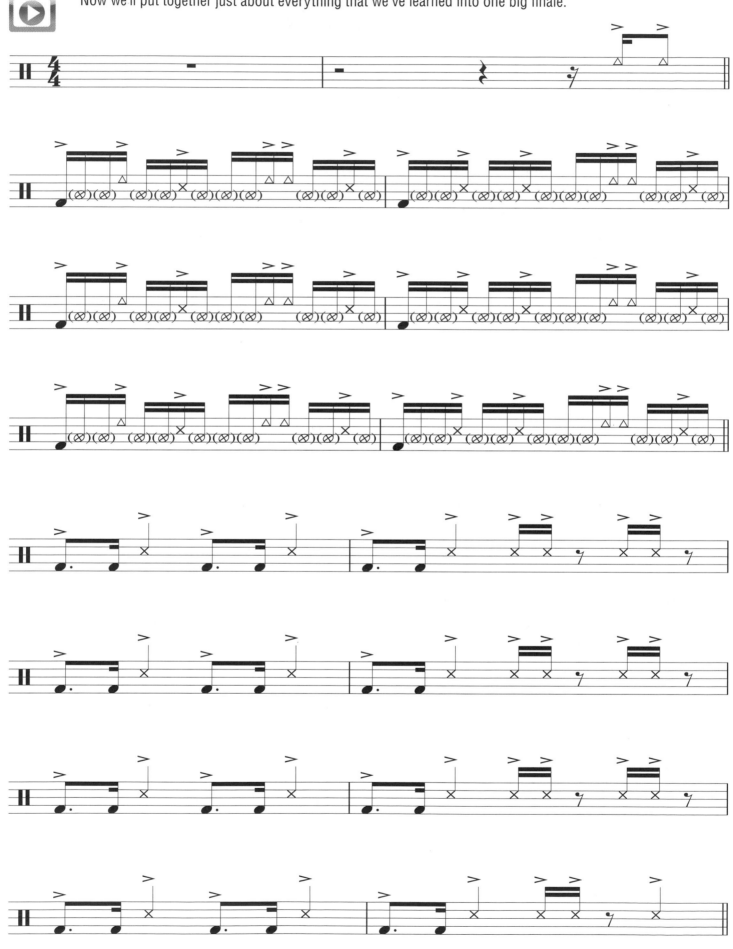

Congratulations! You've now completed the Hal Leonard Cajon Method. You should feel very proud of yourself. You're now playing at an intermediate level and are ready to take your playing even further.

EXCEPTIONAL CAJONS

from *tycoon* ®

PERCUSSION

SUPREMO SERIES HARDWOOD CAJON

The 29 Series Hardwood Box Cajon is constructed of durable and excellent sounding hardwood with a spruce playing surface. It yields deep bass tones and sharp high slaps, with fully adjustable snares. Each cajon is individually handmade and tested to ensure superior sound quality.

00750307 ....$99.00

SUPREMO SELECT DARK IRIS SERIES CAJON

Individually hand-made and tested to ensure superior sound quality, this cajon features a Dark Iris body. It has adjustable snare wires and includes an Allen wrench.

00142593 ....$129.00

CRATE CAJON
29CM

The body of this cajon is constructed of environmentally-friendly Siam oak, with exotic Asian hardwood and Siam oak front plates delivering superb tonal qualities. The hand-carved markings and wooden slats lined across the sides provide a distinct look and feel. Each cajon is individually hand-made and tested to ensure superior sound quality such as deep, loud bass tones and high, sharp slap tones. Includes a snare adjusting Allen wrench.

00755730 ....$174.00

PRACTICE CAJON

This cajon is designed for the player to practice and play with their favorite tracks. Just plug an MP3 player in the input jack and play along to the music! The front plate and body is constructed of environmentally-friendly Siam oak, and the cajon is easily transportable. It's powered by one 9V battery, and the snare wires are adjustable with the included Allen wrench.

00755234 ....$185.00

29 SERIES BUBINGA CAJON – MAKAH BURL FRONT PLATE

Individually hand-made and tested to ensure superior sound quality, this cajon has a Bubinga body and a Makah Burl front plate. Includes a snare-adjusting Allen wrench.

00755227 ....$199.00

35 ROUNDBACK SERIES CAJON – NORTH AMERICAN ASH FRONT PLATE

This special cajon features a curved back panel which provides for superior bass tones. The adjustable snares allow players to tune their cajon with the included allen wrench. The North American ash front panel provides enhanced acoustic tonal qualities.

13.75" x 20.5" front plate.
00755241 ....$249.00

VERTEX SERIES CAJON – AMERICA ASH BODY AND ZEBRANO FRONT PLATE

This innovative ca combines the sharp s of a 29 series cajon the rich bass tones of a series cajon. The un pyramid shape is desig for improved ergonor and comfort, and the b is American ash with a Zebrano front plate. There is enhanced "sweet spot" for added resonance on deep tones. Includes snare-adjusting Allen wrench.
00755244 ....$259

32 SERIES DOHC CAJON

This unique ca contains two sepa chambers and so holes, providing versatile combina of deep, traditic bass sounds and cr tight, snare slaps. body and front p are constructed environmentally-frier Siam oak wood, and rubber feet offer ad stability when playing.
00755257 ....$299

TRIPLE-PLAY CAJON

A first of its kind, an all-in-one cajon designed to prod a great variation of cajon styles and sounds together in drum features three distinctive playing surfaces each produc different sounds.
00142629 ....$359

tycoon ®
PERCUSSION